Original title:
Scars of Strength

Copyright © 2024 Swan Charm
All rights reserved.

Author: Eliora Lumiste
ISBN HARDBACK: 978-9916-89-760-7
ISBN PAPERBACK: 978-9916-89-761-4
ISBN EBOOK: 978-9916-89-762-1

The Heart's Mosaic of Trials

In the quiet whispers of dawn's light,
A soul finds strength, rising from the night.
With every tear, a lesson unfolds,
As faith in the heart silently holds.

Through valleys deep, and mountains high,
Each struggle shapes, as shadows pry.
In the forge of trials, we seek and strive,
A testament to the will to survive.

The hand of grace will guide the way,
Through stormy seas and skies of gray.
In surrender, we find our peace,
A radiant love that will not cease.

With every heartbeat, a story told,
Of hope and redemption, brave and bold.
Embracing the scars that mark the soul,
In the mosaic, we become whole.

So let us walk this sacred path,
With steadfast hearts, embracing the wrath.
For in the trials, we rise anew,
In the heart's mosaic, our spirits imbue.

Triumph Through Tear-stained Halls

In halls where echoes whisper fears,
We tread through paths of ancient tears.
With every step, the heart withstands,
Guided by faith, we clasp His hands.

Though shadows loom, and doubts arise,
We lift our gaze toward hopeful skies.
From sorrow's grip, the spirit soars,
For love's embrace forever roars.

With every trial, the soul refines,
Through tear-stained walls, His light defines.
In moments bleak, His grace reveals,
The strength of heart, the truth that heals.

Testaments of the Tried

In crucibles of fire and pain,
The tried walk paths where courage reigns.
With weary hands, they forge a song,
Of faith unbreakable and strong.

Each test a page, a story told,
Of hope ignited, a heart of gold.
In silent nights, they find their tune,
Beneath the watchful, guiding moon.

Through valleys deep, their voices rise,
In grateful praise, to piercing skies.
For every wound a wisdom sown,
In trials faced, God's paths are known.

Light Beyond the Shadows

When darkness falls and spirits wane,
The heart recalls the sacred name.
In whispered prayers, the soul ignites,
A beacon found in darkest nights.

Through shadows deep, the truth gleams bright,
In faith we find our guiding light.
With every dawn, the promise clear,
The Savior's love dispels all fear.

From struggle's edge, the heart ascends,
To heights where grace and mercy blend.
Embraced by light, we rise anew,
In every breath, His love shines through.

Grace in the Fracture

In fractured hearts and shattered dreams,
A gentle hope, like sunlight, beams.
Through cracks, the grace of love flows wide,
Restoring faith that time denied.

Each piece a lesson, every scar,
A testament of who we are.
In brokenness, His beauty grows,
A tapestry of love that shows.

For every fall, a hand extends,
To lift the weary, broken friends.
In grace, we find our strength anew,
Through fractured paths, His love is true.

The Sacred Journey of Resilience

In the darkness, faith ignites,
Guiding souls through endless nights.
With each step, burdens lightened,
Hearts embraced, by love enlightened.

Mountains rise, shadows fall,
Yet in spirit, we stand tall.
With every trial, strength is born,
In the silence, hope is worn.

Through the storms, we brave the tide,
With grace and courage as our guide.
Every wound, a testament true,
In the sacred path, we renew.

In stillness, whispers draw near,
Reminders cherished, lost in fear.
Forged in fire, united we rise,
With unwavering faith, we reach the skies.

Life's journey is a winding road,
But in resilience, we find our abode.
Together we journey, hand in hand,
In this sacred quest, we understand.

Wounds as Wonders

In the depths of darkest pain,
A glimmer shines like gentle rain.
Every wound a story tells,
Of battles fought and sacred spells.

Nature's brush strokes the heart's scars,
Transforming hurt to healing stars.
In brokenness, beauty unfolds,
A tapestry of life retold.

Through the ashes, new blooms rise,
In wounded soil, spirit flies.
Each fracture mends with gentle grace,
As love's embrace finds its place.

With every tear, wisdom flows,
Through valleys deep, our courage grows.
Wounds are wonders, blessings held,
In every soul, a tale compelled.

We gather strength from lessons learned,\nFrom the fires where passions burned.
In holy trust, we find our way,
Wounds as wonders, come what may.

The Cathedral of Conquered Pain

Within these walls of haunted light,
Echoes linger from the night.
Every heart bears a solemn tale,
In shadows deep, we will not fail.

The steeple rises, dreams take flight,
Carved from loss, crafted in might.
In every crack, love's song resounds,
In suffering, the spirit found.

The altar stands where prayers ascend,
In sacred spaces, hearts will mend.
With every tear, redemption's sign,
Glistening hope, forever divine.

Through turbulent storms, we find our grace,
In the cathedral, we embrace.
Conquered pain, a guiding thread,
Binding us, where angels tread.

Here in the silence, wisdom breathes,
In trusting hearts, true peace we weave.
The cathedral stands, strong and clear,
With conquered pain, we draw near.

Holy Armor of Experience

In life's battle, we don our shield,
With every trial, we dare not yield.
Forged through storms, resilient we stand,
With holy armor, hand in hand.

Each scar a badge, each bruise a sign,
Of journeys walked, paths intertwine.
In every challenge, strength we gain,
The holy armor, born from pain.

With courage, we rise through tempest's breath,
Defying doubt, conquering death.
Our spirits rise, emboldened and true,
In the holy armor, we are renewed.

Through sacred grace, we find our way,
In love's embrace, we choose to stay.
Every lesson, a precious gift,
In experience, our spirits lift.

Together, we wear this armor bright,
Reflection of our inner light.
In unity, we learn to soar,
With holy armor, forevermore.

Fragments of Truth in Tempests

In storms that rage, we seek the light,
Fragments of truth break through the night.
Heavenly whispers within the pain,
Guiding our hearts to rise again.

Each wave a lesson, each tear a prayer,
Trusting the journey, though hard to bear.
In chaos, we find a sacred song,
With faith as our anchor, we can be strong.

Through thunder's roar and lightning's blaze,
Hope rekindles in the darkest days.
The fragments unite, an eternal seam,
Sewing our souls with a flickering dream.

Our hearts are boats on this turbulent sea,
Carried by currents to set us free.
With every tempest, there's truth we earn,
A flicker of grace in the tides we turn.

Resurrection of the Wounded Heart

Amidst the ashes, a spark shall rise,
The wounded heart sheds its disguise.
In the garden of grief, seeds of hope,
Beneath winds of sorrow, we learn to cope.

With each broken shard, the spirit mends,
A sacred promise that never ends.
The tears we've shed, a cleansing flood,
In every drop, a drop of blood.

From darkness, we emerge into the light,
Resurrected souls take their flight.
The burdened chest now breathes anew,
With strength reborn, we rise and pursue.

The love that binds us, forever spark,
Transforms the fear into a prayer, a lark.
In the silence, hear the echoes call,
The wounded heart shall heal through it all.

The Sacred Dance of Imperfection

In the waltz of life, we sway and spin,
Embracing flaws that dwell within.
Each misstep teaches, each stumble sings,
The sacred dance where grace takes wings.

With hearts wide open, we each confess,
Our imperfections, a shared caress.
The beauty blooms in every scar,
Reminding us who we truly are.

In every crack, light finds its way,
Through brokenness, we learn to play.
We twirl in shadows, we leap in grace,
Finding our rhythm in this sacred space.

The fears that bind us, we cast aside,
As love unites, and we choose to glide.
Together we dance, hand in hand,
In the sacredness of this imperfect land.

Forgiveness in the Frayed Edges

In frayed edges, love begins to weave,
Threads of mercy that we receive.
Each whispered word becomes a balm,
Soothing our souls with an endless calm.

Forgiveness is the bridge we cross,
A gentle act that counts no cost.
In the unraveling, we find our way,
Through pain to peace, to light of day.

With open hearts, we stitch the seams,
Mending the fabric of broken dreams.
In every tear, a lesson learned,
In every heartache, the fire burned.

The frayed edges tell stories deep,
Of journeys taken, and promises to keep.
With every fiber, love grows strong,
In forgiveness, we find where we belong.

The Light in Each Crack

In shadows deep, we find our way,
A flicker bright, through night and day.
Each crack a gift, where hope does gleam,
In brokenness, we dare to dream.

With whispers soft, the spirits guide,
In darkest hours, they won't deride.
A gentle touch, in twilight's hue,
They lead us forth, to love anew.

As morning breaks, the light cascades,
In every heart, the truth invades.
Through trials faced, and burdens borne,
We rise again, by grace reborn.

In unity, our voices soar,
Through every crack, we are restored.
Faith lights the path, where shadows flee,
In every heart, the light will be.

So let us walk, with heads held high,
In cracks of stone, the heavens sigh.
With every step, our spirits dance,
Embracing hope, we take our chance.

Unsung Lullabies of Survival

In gentle verses, whispers flow,
Of weary hearts, where sorrows grow.
Each night unfurls, a tale untold,
In shadows dim, we find our gold.

The cry of souls, both lost and found,
In silent nights, our truths resound.
Unseen angels, guide our dreams,
Through tangled paths, they weave their seams.

Against the storms, our spirits rise,
In the stillness, see the skies.
Each lullaby, a sacred trust,
In hope's embrace, we find what's just.

With every breath, we sing the songs,
Of battles fought, where we belong.
Through unseen trials, we learn to stand,
In unity, we take each hand.

Let not the shadows dim our light,
For in our hearts, we hold the fight.
Together strong, we face the night,
With lullabies of love so bright.

Tapestry of the Trials

Each thread we weave, a story spun,
In colors bold, the battles won.
A tapestry, of joy and pain,
Through tears and laughter, wisdom gained.

In darkest hours, the fabric sways,
As faith is tested, through the days.
Each moment stitched, a lesson learned,
In each heart's fire, the spirit burned.

With hands of grace, we shape our fate,
In every knot, the power of late.
Through trials faced, we've come to know,
In love's embrace, the gardens grow.

As colors blend, and shadows teem,
We find our strength in the shared dream.
In every stitch, a prayer is cast,
With hope combined, we rise at last.

Together, we create the art,
Of lives entwined, of sacred heart.
In life's great weave, we find our place,
In every trial, a touch of grace.

Redemption in the Ruins

Among the stones, where dreams once lay,
A whisper calls, to light the way.
In ruins deep, we seek the spark,
To guide us forth, through the dark.

In broken hearts, redemption flows,
From ashes rise, the hope that grows.
With eyes wide open, we dare to see,
In every crack, still beauty be.

Through shattered paths, we walk anew,
Embracing light, with every hue.
Each scar a mark, of battles won,
In every soul, God's will be done.

The past may haunt, but we move on,
In ruins old, the dawn is drawn.
With faith as wings, through pain we soar,
In every loss, we find the shore.

So stand with me, in this vast space,
For in our hearts, we hold His grace.
Redemption blooms, where hope ignites,
In ruins fading, love's light shines bright.

Celestial Fractures of Faith

In the shadows, whispers dwell,
Questions linger, souls do swell.
Torn between the light and dark,
Faint embers of a holy spark.

Bridges built on sacred ground,
Where the lost and found are bound.
Through the storms, the heart must soar,
In the silence, hear the roar.

Every prayer like fragments shed,
Each tear, a voice, a broken thread.
Yet hope, like stars, will shine so bright,
Guiding seekers through the night.

From the dust, we rise again,
Chasing shadows of past sin.
In the fractures, grace remains,
Healing wounds, dissolving chains.

Celestial truths from ancient scrolls,
Whisper peace to thirsty souls.
In the depths of doubt and fear,
Faith will lead, forever near.

Celestial Marks of Transition

A dawn breaks slow, the heavens hum,
Silent songs of what's to come.
Footsteps falter on life's frame,
Every instant, never the same.

In the stillness, spirits rise,
Transcending darkness, touching skies.
Marks of time on weary hearts,
Every ending, new start imparts.

Wings of change, a gentle breeze,
Calling forth from knees to seize.
Cycles weave through life's grand dance,
In the turning, find romance.

Voices echo through the air,
Whispers of love, laced with prayer.
Journey forth, for paths are wide,
In each moment, grace will guide.

Celestial signs adorn the way,
Guiding pilgrims, come what may.
Each transition, a holy sign,
In the soul, the stars align.

Elysium's Mark

In the garden, blooms arise,
Painted with the softest skies.
Every petal, story told,
Of lives lived brave, of hearts bold.

Waves of light dance on the sea,
Carrys whispers, wild and free.
Elysium, a sacred space,
Where spirits dwell, embraced by grace.

With each step on hallowed ground,
Elysium's serenade, profound.
The air alive with soulful sighs,
Hearts ignited, reaching high.

Stars above in endless glow,
Mark the paths that seekers go.
In the silence, hear the call,
Elysium waits, for one and all.

Infinite love wraps around,
In this haven, peace is found.
With every breath, the spirit's claim,
Elysium, forever reigns.

The Sacred Dance of the Deformed

In shadows deep, where heartbeats fold,
The deformed find grace, their stories told.
With every step, in silence they sway,
Dancing through darkness, they light the way.

A chorus of souls, each flaw a gem,
In unity they rise, rejecting the condemn.
With hands outstretched, they reach for the sky,
Transforming despair, their spirits fly.

In the sacred circle, they twist and turn,
Embracing the fire, for love they yearn.
The dance of the deformed calls all to see,
That beauty thrives in what cannot be free.

In whispers of twilight, they gather near,
A testament of faith, dissolving fear.
With every heartbeat, in rhythm divine,
The sacred dance binds, where hearts intertwine.

So let us join hands, with love as our guide,
In the dance of the deformed, may we abide.
For in every angle and curve, we find,
The sacred truth that unites all mankind.

Shepherding Through the Shadows

In fields of sorrow, the shepherd stands,
Guiding the lost with gentle hands.
Through valleys of pain, he walks the path,
With love as his staff, and grace as his math.

The shadows lengthen, but hope remains,
In every heartbeat, in all our pains.
Each soul a lamb, in need of care,
He lifts them high, with love to share.

Through storms that rage and winds that howl,
The shepherd calls, with a comforting growl.
In darkness they gather, united in prayer,
Finding solace in trust, no weight too bear.

With eyes of compassion, he sees our plight,
Comforting hearts through the long, dark night.
For every burden, he bears the weight,
In shepherding shadows, he opens the gate.

When dawn arrives, with light and song,
The shepherd rejoices, we all belong.
Together we rise, through joy and strife,
In the embrace of love, we find our life.

Eternity's Embrace of the Wounded

The wounded wander, in search of grace,
In each broken heart, a sacred space.
With hands outstretched, they reach for the light,
In eternity's embrace, they find their might.

Every scar a story, each tear a prayer,
In the silence of night, we hear their fare.
For wounds reveal the path to the soul,
In the dance of healing, we become whole.

In shadows we gather, with whispers so soft,
The wounded held high, like spirits aloft.
Together we rise, with courage anew,
In eternity's embrace, we are born true.

Through valleys of sorrow, we walk as one,
In the light of dawn, our fears come undone.
With hearts intertwined, we face the day,
In the warmth of love, we find our way.

So let us remember, in joy and strife,
The beauty of wounds, a part of our life.
In eternity's embrace, we find our home,
Together we flourish, never alone.

The Beatitudes of Brokenness

Blessed are the broken, in shambles they stand,
For in their frailty, they hold the land.
Through tears they sow seeds of grace and peace,
In their humble hearts, all judgments cease.

Blessed are the weary, the burdened with care,
For in their weariness, love will repair.
With each soft whisper, of comfort drawn near,
Their spirits awaken, vanquishing fear.

Blessed are the lost, who wander alone,
For in their journey, they'll find their home.
In every misstep, and every fall,
They rise with resilience, answering the call.

Blessed are the meek, their strength in restraint,
For through their compassion, they show what they paint.

With arms wide open, they gather our pain,
In the beatitudes' embrace, love will reign.

So let us rejoice in our brokenness here,
For in our fragility, God draws near.
Through the beatitudes, we learn to see,
That brokenness binds us, eternally free.

Beneath the Shattered Halo

Beneath the shattered halo's light,
We gather in the dim twilight.
With hope we seek a path anew,
In faith, our hearts must break through.

From ashes rise the souls once lost,
In trials we endure the cost.
Each tear becomes a sacred prayer,
In love divine, we breathe the air.

The echoes of our silent cries,
Are heard by him who never lies.
With every wound, a lesson learned,
In grace's warmth, we are returned.

The shattered pieces on the ground,
Reflect the beauty that we've found.
In unity, our spirits soar,
For in our pain, we are much more.

So let us walk this road as one,
Until our journey here is done.
With every step, we're bound by light,
In darkness, faith will shine so bright.

Forged in Fire's Embrace

In fire's embrace, the soul is tried,
Through trials fierce, we won't divide.
From molten depths, we rise anew,
Transformed by flames, our spirits grew.

Each scar a testament of grace,
We find our strength in toughened space.
With every burn, a story told,
In faith we trust, though hearts feel cold.

The furnace of our darkest days,
Reveals the light in myriad ways.
With every dawn, we brave the storm,
In love's embrace, we are reborn.

The heat may bend but never break,
For in our hearts, the trust we make.
Provision comes from trials faced,
In fire's embrace, we've been graced.

So let the flames of life ignite,
Our spirits high, our vision bright.
Together, strong, we rise and stand,
Forged in fire, united hand in hand.

Wounds of the Faithful Heart

Wounds of the faithful heart run deep,
Yet in our suffering, we shall keep.
Each pang a reminder of love's call,
Through trials faced, we stand tall.

The burdens borne are lifted high,
In prayerful whispers, we rely.
Each tear transforms our heavy load,
In hope's embrace, we find our road.

Amidst the fray, we sense the grace,
That flows from every wounded place.
For through the pain, our spirits mend,
In sorrow's depths, we find a friend.

Let us not haste in seeking light,
For wounded hearts can still take flight.
In faith we walk; we grow in trust,
Through love, our ashes turn to dust.

And in this journey, hand in hand,
Our faithful hearts together stand.
With wounds that heal, our souls will soar,
In unity, we are much more.

The Test of Broken Vessels

The test of broken vessels shines,
Through cracks and chips, the light defines.
Each flaw a mark of how we've grown,
In our journeys, seeds are sown.

From emptiness, we learn to fill,
With kindness, grace, and boundless will.
A vessel strong may still be cracked,
But in our hearts, love's never lacked.

We carry burdens, great and small,
Yet in our weakness, we stand tall.
In shattered forms, we bear the truth,
For faith restores the heart of youth.

Let brokenness not bring us shame,
But be the spark that fuels the flame.
For in this trial, we find our place,
In perfect union with divine grace.

So raise the vessels, let them sing,
In harmony, our voices ring.
Through brokenness, we come alive,
In love's embrace, our spirits thrive.

Graces of the Bruised

In shadows deep, where sorrows lie,
There blooms a grace, a silent sigh.
The bruised heart learns, with tender might,
To rise anew, embracing light.

Each tear a gem, each wound a song,
In weakness found, we now belong.
The hands that lift us, guide our way,
Through darkest nights to brightest day.

With faith as balm, our spirits soar,
The bruised are blessed, forevermore.
In every crack, His light will seep,
Awakening love, our souls to keep.

So hold the pain, for in its cost,
We find the path to what was lost.
The grace we seek is born of strife,
In every bruise, we find our life.

Thus walk we on, our burden shared,
In love's embrace, we are prepared.
With hope as anchor, hearts will mend,
In graces true, we find our end.

The Blessed and the Broken

In every heart where shadows dwell,
A story weaves, a sacred spell.
The blessed know well of earth's embrace,
While broken souls still seek His grace.

The hands that hold, both cracked and warm,
In gentle strength, break every storm.
For every struggle speaks His name,
In whispered prayers, we share the flame.

They walk a path, both rough and bright,
In every stumble, found in light.
The blessed and broken, side by side,
In unity, our hearts abide.

So let us stand, in love's great fray,
With open arms, come what may.
For in our wounds, His healing lent,
The broken are forever meant.

With grateful hearts, we sing and rise,
In every tear, a sacred prize.
The blessed, the broken, intertwined,
In love's embrace, our peace defined.

Folded Prayers in Pain

In quiet nights, when shadows fall,
We fold our hands, we heed the call.
In whispered words, our hearts will plead,
For solace found in every need.

The pain we carry, heavy yet light,
Transforms to whispers, entwined with might.
Each prayer a thread, both soft and strong,
Woven in faith, we all belong.

As tears descend, they wash the soul,
In every struggle, He makes us whole.
The folded prayers, like lilies bloom,
In midst of darkness, dispelling gloom.

In silent breaths, with eyes raised high,
We find the strength to still comply.
For pain may linger, but hope remains,
In folded prayers, our heart sustains.

So let us kneel, in trust we stand,
With folded prayers, in His great hand.
Through every trial, and every strain,
We rise again, from folded pain.

Holy Inscription of the Heart

In every beat, a tale unfolds,
Of love divine, of truths retold.
The holy inscription, written in grace,
An echoing promise in time and space.

Amid the storms and trials we face,
This heart, a vessel, holds His embrace.
With joy and sorrow, we find our part,
In every moment, the sacred art.

Each line inscribed with tears and laughter,
Reflects the path that leads hereafter.
For in our hearts, His words remain,
A testament through joy and pain.

In silent prayers, we seek to heal,
A canvas adorned, a sacred seal.
In holy whispers, our spirits soar,
In each inscription, we are restored.

So read with care the lines we've penned,
In love's embrace, our souls transcend.
For every heart, a tale of art,
In holy inscription, we find our start.

The Lamp of Perseverance

In the shadow of despair, we stand,
With faith as our guiding hand.
Through trials that test our soul,
The lamp of hope keeps us whole.

Every step on the rugged way,
Brings light to the darkened day.
With each struggle, our spirits rise,
In perseverance, our heart complies.

Though storms may rage and winds may howl,
In the night, we hear the owl.
Its wisdom speaks of strength divine,
Through every test, the stars align.

Our prayers ascend like fragrant smoke,
In silence, the heart may invoke.
With unwavering trust, we endure,
The path ahead, steadfast and sure.

So let the lamp of courage burn,
In every corner, let us learn.
With faith unshaken, we will trod,
Each step a testament to God.

Reverent Suffering

In quiet pain, we find our way,
Each tear a prayer, a holy stay.
The trials faced with reverent grace,
In suffering, we seek His face.

With every wound, a lesson comes,
We hear the beat of holy drums.
Through hurt, we rise, our voices strong,
In reverent suffering, we belong.

The night is deep, yet stars will gleam,
In anguish, we cling to the dream.
For in the valley, we learn to kneel,
In faith's embrace, our hearts shall heal.

Each sacrifice points to the light,
In brokenness, we reach for sight.
The cross we bear is not in vain,
For joy will blossom through the pain.

Let us not shun the weight we bear,
For in each trial, He's always there.
With reverent hearts, we boldly tread,
In the path of love, we are led.

The Altar of Adversity

In trials that bring us to our knees,
We build an altar, hearts at ease.
With stones of hardship, faith takes form,
In adversity, our spirits warm.

A sacred space where burdens rest,
In every struggle, we are blessed.
With each sacrifice, we rise anew,
The altar teaches, the heart breaks through.

In shadows cast by doubt and fear,
Our prayers ascend, they draw Him near.
With humbled hearts, we make our plea,
For strength in weakness, we long to be.

The fire of trials ignites the soul,
In its embrace, we become whole.
Each moment of pain, a holy vow,
At the altar, we learn to bow.

Through adversity, our spirits soar,
In every crack, the light will pour.
We find His grace in every tear,
At the altar, love conquers fear.

Miracles Born of Tribulation

In the darkest hour, a whisper calls,
From the depths of struggle, faith enthralls.
Through trials faced in silent strife,
Miracles bloom, breathing new life.

Against the odds, we rise and stand,
With faith unyielding, hand in hand.
Through tribulation, the spirit's wrought,
A tapestry of hope is sought.

From ashes, we gather strength anew,
In every hardship, love shines through.
Each miracle forms in the mire,
Kindled by the heart's desire.

With eyes afire, we watch and see,
The beauty born of suffering's plea.
In every trial, God's hand is near,
Miracles flourish in quiet cheer.

So let us dance upon the pain,
With grateful hearts, we shall not feign.
For in tribulation's sacred song,
Miracles rise, where we belong.

A Testament of Trials and Triumph

In shadows deep where silence dwells,
The spirit cries, yet hope compels.
With faith as light, I tread the way,
Each hardship faced, a step to pray.

The mountains rise, the valleys low,
Through storms that rage, our hearts still glow.
In every tear, a lesson learned,
With every scar, the spirit burned.

From bitter roots, sweet fruits do spring,
In trials faced, our souls take wing.
With hands outstretched, we find the grace,
In every challenge, love's embrace.

Together strong, we lift each other,
In unity, we find a mother.
For in each trial, strength is gained,
Through every loss, the heart unchained.

So rise we shall, our voices clear,
In testament of faith, we steer.
For every trial that we face,
Is but a step toward higher grace.

Cleansing Fires of Worth

In flames that dance, the spirit grows,
Through every trial, the essence flows.
The embers spark, igniting light,
In darkest hours, we seek the bright.

Cleansed by fire, the heart reveals,
Strength refined, the soul it heals.
From ashes, hope shall rise anew,
In every trial, a vision true.

The furnace hot, yet faith withstands,
With gentle grace, we join our hands.
In trials faced, our worth we gain,
From every loss, resilience reigns.

The light within begins to shine,
In sacred trust, our hearts align.
Through cleansing fires, we find our way,
In every dawn, a brand new day.

So let us walk through storms of grace,
With courage strong, we stand in place.
For in our hearts, the fire shall blaze,
A testament to worth that stays.

The Artistry of Surviving Grace

In brushstrokes bold, our lives unfold,
With colors bright, through tales retold.
Each stroke a struggle, each hue a fight,
In artistry, we find our light.

For every shadow that we face,
A masterpiece of love and grace.
The canvas wide, our spirits soar,
In every struggle, we find the core.

From whispered doubts to shouts of pride,
In artistry, we shall abide.
Though tempests rage and waters rise,
A song of hope beneath the skies.

With every tear, a brushstroke clear,
The beauty formed from all we fear.
Resilience blooms in heart's embrace,
In every trial, we find our place.

So let us paint with colors bright,
Our lives a tapestry of light.
For in the art of surviving grace,
We create a world, a sacred space.

Threads of Strength Woven in Tears

From weary hearts, the threads are spun,
In every tear, the strength begun.
Through trials faced, the fabric grows,
In woven lives, the truth bestows.

Each thread a story, rich and deep,
In whispered prayers, our souls do keep.
With every knot, a bond is formed,
Through testing times, our spirits warmed.

Resilient we, through storms and strife,
In woven grace, we weave our life.
The tapestry tells of love so vast,
In every struggle, we are cast.

Together strong, we hold the line,
In unity, our hearts align.
For in our seams, the strength we find,
In every tear, love intertwined.

So let us cherish every strand,
In every thread, a gentle hand.
For through the tears and trials' dance,
We find our strength, our sacred chance.

The Celestial Hand of Recovery

In darkness deep, a light appears,
A gentle touch, calming fears.
Through trials faced, the spirit bends,
The hand of grace, our hearts it mends.

With faith anew, we rise to heal,
Our wounds exposed, the truth revealed.
In whispers soft, the angels sing,
Restoring hope, in them we cling.

The road is long, yet love will guide,
A brother's strength, stand side by side.
In every tear, a lesson found,
The celestial hand, forever bound.

Through stormy trials, our souls refined,
In unity, our hearts aligned.
With each small step, we find our way,
The light within will never sway.

Virtues Born from Pain

From shattered dreams, new strength is born,
In autumn's chill, we greet the dawn.
Through aching hearts, compassion grows,
The seeds of grace, our spirit sows.

Patience learned, in fire we stand,
With humble hearts, we reach for land.
Forgiveness blooms from hurtful strife,
In fragile moments, we find life.

The burdens carried, trials faced,
Each painful step has love embraced.
In suffering's depths, we learn to rise,
With open hearts, we touch the skies.

Together bound, we seek the light,
Each bruise and scar, a path made bright.
In virtues forged amidst the pain,
Resilience born, forever reigns.

The Prayer of the Wounded

Oh, gentle Lord, hear my plea,
In every wound, I call to thee.
With heavy heart and spirit tried,
I seek the peace that you provide.

Through tears I shed, your love I seek,
In silent cries, my soul grows weak.
Each whispered prayer, a cry for grace,
In warmth divine, I find my place.

Restore my strength, ignite the flame,
In brokenness, I seek your name.
Beneath the weight of all my fears,
I lift my heart, and dry the tears.

For in the dark, you walk with me,
In pain's embrace, you set me free.
Through all my trials, I still believe,
In mercy's arms, I shall receive.

Seraphic Signs of Perseverance

In trials faced, we see the signs,
With every step, a love that shines.
Through aching nights and weary days,
The seraphs guide our troubled ways.

With wings of light, they lift us high,
A silent prayer upon the sky.
In darkest moments, hope ignites,
With seraphic signs, we win the fights.

Each challenge met is strength refined,
In battles fought, our souls aligned.
Through faith bestowed, we rise again,
With every loss, a chance to gain.

Though weary hearts may ache and break,
The path is clear, no more forsake.
In perseverance, we find our way,
In seraphic signs, we trust and stay.

Resilience Beneath Heaven's Gaze

Beneath the stars we tread our path,
With burdens small, or heavy wrath.
Yet faith ignites the weary heart,
In trials faced, we find our part.

The gentle whispers of the skies,
Remind us, under watchful eyes,
That every tear is not in vain,
For love transforms our grief to gain.

In shadows deep, our spirits rise,
With every fall, we touch the prize.
The strength within, a sacred flame,
Burning bright in heaven's name.

Together we embrace the night,
With steady hands, we seek the light.
For in the struggle, grace is found,
Resilience blooms on sacred ground.

So let our hearts call forth the dawn,
For in our trials, we are reborn.
With heaven's gaze, we stand in faith,
Our spirits strong, no fear of wraith.

Golden Threads of Trial

In woven strands of joy and grief,
Gold glimmers bright beyond belief.
Each challenge faced a thread so pure,
A tapestry that will endure.

Through tempests fierce and raging storms,
We find our strength in sacred forms.
For every test, a lesson learned,
In trials faced, our spirits burned.

The golden threads that bind us tight,
Illuminate through darkest night.
They show the path that's yours and mine,
In shared struggle, we intertwine.

So let us thread the looms of fate,
With courage bold, we navigate.
Each thread a echo of our cries,
In faith we stand, and ever rise.

With every strand a story told,
A testament to hearts so bold.
Our golden threads a holy mark,
Of trials faced, we journeyed far.

Spiritual Tattoos

In silence etched, our stories weave,
Marks of love we hold and grieve.
Each scar a testament of grace,
In sacred ink, we find our place.

These spiritual tattoos we wear,
Speak of battles fought with care.
An imprint deep, a badge of pride,
Through every storm, we never hide.

The flesh remembers what the heart knows,
In every tear, a blossom grows.
In sacred art, we share our pain,
From loss, our deepest strength we gain.

So let the world see every mark,
For in our wounds, we leave a spark.
With each design, a heart laid bare,
In love, we find the strength to share.

These spiritual tattoos tell our tale,
Through every struggle, we prevail.
In sacred ink, our journeys flow,
A tapestry of life's great glow.

The Blessed Burden

Oh, blessed burden that we bear,
In heavy hearts, our truths laid bare.
Each weight a gift, though hard to see,
A path to light, a way to be.

Through valleys deep and mountains high,
We carry forth, we do not sigh.
For strength awakens in the trial,
In every tear, we find a smile.

The burden shared is lightened grace,
In faith, our struggles find their place.
With every step, we rise to meet,
The sacred call, our souls entreat.

So let us lift each other high,
With hearts united, we defy.
The blessed burden, a sacred trust,
In love we flourish, rise and thrust.

With every challenge faced in prayer,
We blossom bright beyond despair.
In burdens borne, our truth is found,
In every heartbeat, love profound.

Mosaic of the Redeemed

Each shard of broken glass,
Reflects a story bright,
In the hands of the Master,
Transformed into pure light.

Out of ashes, beauty blooms,
In the depths of despair,
Faith weaves a tapestry,
Of love beyond compare.

Grace cascades like a waterfall,
Washing sins away,
In the heart of the faithful,
Hope begins to sway.

With every tear that's shed,
A seed of joy is sown,
Through trials and tribulations,
We never walk alone.

Mosaic of the Redeemed,
United in His grace,
We rise amid the shadows,
Revealing Heaven's face.

Gifts Wrapped in Suffering

In the winter's harsh embrace,
A bud begins to grow,
Wrapped in layers of sorrow,
A gift from down below.

Pain carves a deeper faith,
Like a sculptor's careful hand,
Molding hearts into vessels,
Ready to understand.

Through the night of anguish,
A spark of hope ignites,
For each wound and each struggle,
Brings forth victorious sights.

When the burden feels too much,
And shadows fill the day,
Remember in the darkness,
Gifts of love will stay.

Emerging from the trial,
With treasures that we claim,
In suffering, we discover,
Life's beautiful refrain.

The Disciple's Journey through Pain

Upon the rugged pathway,
The burdens oft grow steep,
With faith as our compass,
Through valleys, we yet leap.

The cross upon our shoulders,
Reminds us of His grace,
Each step may seem unworthy,
Yet, we seek His face.

In every trial encountered,
A lesson waits to be,
For in the depths of struggle,
We find humility.

The scars that mark our journey,
Are stories of His love,
Each wound a silent witness,
To guidance from above.

Through pain, we grow together,
Bound by a common thread,
Disciples in communion,
Where our souls are led.

Allegiance of the Wounded

In the garden where we kneel,
With hearts both torn and bare,
Wounded souls find refuge,
In the arms of prayer.

We gather in the sunlight,
Sharing tales of our plight,
Each scar a badge of honor,
In the shadowed night.

Through whispers of our struggles,
We form a sacred bond,
Allegiance of the wounded,
A melody beyond.

With healing waters flowing,
We rise, our spirits high,
Together, we are stronger,
As we reach for the sky.

In unity, we stand,
With faith as our decree,
Allegiance of the wounded,
Forever, we will be.

Songs of Resilient Grace

In shadows deep, the spirit sings,
A melody that softly clings,
Through storm and strife, we find our peace,
In grace divine, our fears release.

With every tear, a seed is sown,
In heart's embrace, we are not alone,
The path is long, yet hope remains,
In faith's embrace, we break our chains.

Through trials faced, our voices rise,
A chorus bright that fills the skies,
With steady hearts and hands entwined,
In love's embrace, our souls aligned.

The whispers of the Divine call,
In prayerful strength, we stand tall,
For every wound, a lesson learned,
In moments lost, the light returns.

In every fear, a chance to grow,
Through rugged paths, our spirits flow,
With grace profound, we walk anew,
Embracing all, in gratitude.

Covenant of the Weathered Spirit

In weathered hearts, the promise stays,
A beacon bright through darker days,
With every breath, a vow to keep,
In silent prayers, our souls shall weep.

The battle scars, a badge of grace,
In trials faced, we find our place,
Through shattered dreams, the light will shine,
A sacred bond, divine design.

When earthly ties begin to fray,
We lift our hands, and softly pray,
With open hearts, we welcome change,
In love's embrace, all wounds arrange.

With every storm, a chance to rise,
To storms within, we will not disguise,
For in the dark, our spirits mend,
In unity, our hearts transcend.

Through every dawn, we find our way,
In whispered hopes and bright arrays,
Together bound, we walk the line,
In faith we stand, our spirits shine.

The Altar of Trials and Tribulations

At the altar where we kneel,
Our hearts laid bare, our truths reveal,
With every trial, our spirits grow,
In strength divine, we learn to flow.

With burdens heavy, we question why,
Yet in the dark, our dreams comply,
For every tear that leaves a mark,
A light is born within the dark.

When shadows loom and courage wanes,
In silent breath, the spirit gains,
For each temptation leads us near,
A closer walk, our path made clear.

In every fall, the rise is sweet,
A sacred dance, where fears deplete,
Through trials faced, our strength confirmed,
In every flame, our souls have burned.

So let us gather, hand in hand,
In faith we trust, together stand,
For at this altar, hope ignites,
In every challenge, love unites.

Elysium of the Endured

In Elysium, where spirits soar,
Amidst the trials, we find our core,
With every burden, a gift bestowed,
In sacred ground, our spirits flowed.

Through valleys low and mountains high,
Our hearts are stitched with threads of sky,
In whispered hope, the light will gleam,
A paradise born from every dream.

For in the struggle, we rise anew,
Embracing all in love's sweet view,
With open arms and hearts ablaze,
We dance in joy through endless days.

In moments tough, where shadows creep,
A spark of love, our souls shall keep,
Through every ache, we find our grace,
In Elysium's warm embrace.

So let us wander, side by side,
In faith and love, our hearts abide,
For in the trials, we come to know,
The beauty of the seeds we sow.

Blessings in the Broken

In shattered clay, a potter's grace,
Finding beauty in every trace.
Broken hearts learn to mend,
In cracks, the light will ascend.

A whispered prayer, a gentle sigh,
Hearts of stone begin to fly.
In the silence, hope will bloom,
From the ashes, love finds room.

The broken spirit finds its song,
In the struggle, we belong.
Each fall teaches us to rise,
In our weakness, strength complies.

Gathered pieces, a mosaic bright,
In every shard, a piece of light.
With grace bestowed, we learn to see,
In our scars, we find the key.

Sanctity of the Wounded

In the wounds, a sacred truth,
Healing comes from the heart of youth.
In every tear, a chance to feel,
Wounded souls begin to heal.

The pain we carry, a gentle guide,
Through the shadows, hope will bide.
With every bruise, a story we bear,
In silent whispers, we share our flare.

The sanctum found in our despair,
Holds a promise in every prayer.
Letting go, we learn to trust,
In the brokenness, we find the just.

Rays of light through darkest nights,
Illuminate our inner sights.
In the struggle, we discover grace,
Each wound a mark of love's embrace.

The Sacred Path of Pain

Upon the path, the thorns do grow,
But wisdom springs from seeds we sow.
In every step, a lesson learned,
Through trials faced, our hearts discerned.

The sacred journey, steep and long,
In shadows deep, we find the strong.
Through every trial, our spirits soar,
In pain's embrace, we learn to adore.

With tender hands, we mend the tears,
In silent moments, God's love shares.
The sacred pain, both fierce and true,
Shows us paths that lead anew.

As stars emerge from darkest night,
Our souls ignite with purpose bright.
In struggles shared, together we gain,
Strength to walk the sacred plain.

Celestial Echoes of Endurance

In the cosmos vast, we take our stand,
Celestial whispers guide our hand.
Through trials faced, we find our voice,
In echoing strength, we rejoice.

With every heartbeat, we endure,
The trials known, we face, we cure.
In celestial realms, our souls entwine,
Find the light where stars align.

Through tempest winds, our spirits hoist,
In love resounding, we find our choice.
Each echo heard, a prayer in flight,
In endurance, we embrace the light.

With open hearts, we hold the flame,
In every song, we praise His name.
Through darkest nights, the dawn will break,
In echoes true, our souls awake.

Rebirth in Ruins

In shadows deep, the spirit sighs,
From ashes cold, the heart will rise.
Each broken stone, a tale of grace,
In ruins found, we seek His face.

With every tear, a seed is sown,
In barren lands, His love is known.
Through silent night, the dawn will break,
A new beginning, for His sake.

The path we walk may twist and bend,
Yet in His love, we find a friend.
Each step of faith, so brave and bold,
In rubble's grasp, His truth unfolds.

From every loss, a lesson learned,
In brokenness, our hearts have turned.
He guides us through the darkest days,
In every heart, His light displays.

In ruins still, we stand and pray,
For in His arms, we find our way.
Rebirth awaits, through faith we see,
In every ruin, He sets us free.

Redemption Through Trials

Through trials faced, the soul expands,
In struggles deep, He holds our hands.
Each burden borne, a step toward peace,
Redemption waits, and fears will cease.

With every storm, our faith ignites,
In darkest hours, His love unites.
We rise, we fall, yet still we strive,
Through every test, our spirits thrive.

His whispers guide through pain and doubt,
In trials fierce, His strength we tout.
Each scar a mark of battles won,
In shadowed paths, we behold the sun.

The fire burns, but gold remains,
In every loss, His joy sustains.
A journey fraught with lessons learned,
Through trials vast, our hearts are turned.

Faith forged in strife, we stand anew,
In brokenness, His love shines through.
Redemption sings, in pain we're grown,
Through trials faced, His grace is shown.

Embracing the Ashen

In ashes deep, we find our worth,
From charred remains, emerges birth.
Each ember speaks of flames endured,
In ashen lands, our hearts are stirred.

We gather strength from smoky gray,
In silence, wisdom paves the way.
Through shattered dreams and fading light,
We hold the shadows close, yet bright.

The ashen paths, a sacred space,
To find in stillness, God's embrace.
In quiet whispers, hope takes flight,
From settled dust, we rise in light.

Each crack reflects a story told,
In fragile strength, our faith is bold.
Embrace the ash, its lessons true,
In every ending, life anew.

So let us walk through ashen lands,
With open hearts and willing hands.
For in the dark, His light we find,
Embracing all, in love entwined.

Trials That Make Us Whole

In trials faced, we seek the truth,
In every challenge, lies our youth.
From burdens borne, our spirits grow,
Through winding paths, His grace we know.

Each struggle shaped with care and might,
In darkest days, we find the light.
Through fierce tests, our souls are honed,
In patience held, our hearts atoned.

The path is rough, yet hope remains,
Through every tear, our joy sustains.
In trials met, we find our role,
Through every wound, we are made whole.

With faith as guide, we stand up tall,
In every fall, we heed His call.
Each moment faced, a chance to grow,
In trials that forge, we learn to glow.

And when we rise, renewed in grace,
In every scar, a shining trace.
For trials faced and lessons learned,
In love, our hearts eternally yearned.

The Serpent and the Crocus

In shadows deep, the serpent's glide,
A crocus blooms, with grace to bide.
Whispers of faith in gentle light,
Hope intertwines with the night.

In barren lands where doubts conspire,
The crocus rises, igniting fire.
With every petal, a prayer takes flight,
Defying fears, unveiling right.

The serpent coils, with cunning eyes,
Yet beauty breaks through earthly ties.
In life's embrace, both dark and bright,
The heart will flourish, bold and light.

Where thorns may pierce, and shadows loom,
The crocus speaks, dispelling gloom.
In every struggle, a lesson shared,
With faith, the spirit is prepared.

So let us weave this sacred tale,
Of serpent's hiss and crocus pale.
In nature's rhythm, find the call,
For hope shall rise and never fall.

Testimony of the Scarred Soul

In silence deep, the scarred soul speaks,
With heavy heart, in truth it seeks.
Each wound a story, a path to grace,
In brokenness, the light we trace.

Through trials met, and battles fought,
The scars remind us of lessons taught.
In every tear, a glimpse of dawn,
A testament to love, reborn.

Fractured pieces, yet whole we stand,
In faith's embrace, we join the band.
The scars we bear, a sacred sign,
A journey rich, where spirits shine.

Let not despair enfold your heart,
For from the dark, the light will start.
In unity, our voices rise,
A chorus shared, that never dies.

So lift your eyes, beyond the pain,
With every scar, true strength we gain.
The testimony of the soul we share,
In love's embrace, we find our prayer.

Faiths that Fashion Fortitude

In quiet corners, faith is found,
A sturdy whisper, a holy sound.
Through storms that rage and trials vast,
Fortitude blooms, steadfast and fast.

Each struggle faced, a mark of grace,
In faith's embrace, we find our place.
With courage firm, our spirits rise,
In shadows deep, we claim the prize.

From ancient tales, the wisdom flows,
In every heart, a fire glows.
The faiths we carry, burden shared,
In unity, the brave are spared.

So plant the seeds of hope anew,
Let every prayer guide you through.
With faith as light, and love as key,
We fashion strength, eternally.

Together we stand, in sacred trust,
With faith that flourishes, firm and just.
In each brave step, let joy abound,
In faiths that fashion, the lost are found.

Chronicles of Courage

In tales of old, where heroes dwell,
Chronicles rise, their stories swell.
With every heart that dares to fight,
  Courage ignites, dispelling night.

From whispers soft, to roaring sound,
In trials endured, the truth is found.
With every step upon this road,
The chronicles of courage flowed.

Through mountains high and valleys low,
  The spirit soars, in faith we go.
For every wound that time bestows,
  A strength emerges, the heart knows.

Let not the fears take hold so tight,
For courage shines, a guiding light.
In every chapter, brave souls stand,
  In unity's name, we take a hand.

So weave your stories, bold and true,
In chronicles vast, the old and new.
In every act, let courage sing,
For each small step, great hope can bring.

Benevolent Burdens

From heights above, the burdens fall,
With love embedded, heed the call.
Each weight we carry, grace bestowed,
In trials faced, our spirits grow.

Embrace the path that God has made,
In darkened nights, light will invade.
With every step, a purpose clear,
In burdens shared, we cast out fear.

Upon our hearts, His hands we place,
To lift the load with boundless grace.
Together strong, we find our way,
In giving love, we learn to stay.

Each tear a sign of strength within,
In hardships borne, our souls begin.
A tapestry of pain and joy,
In every thread, our faith employed.

So let us walk this sacred road,
With benevolence, we share the load.
In every burden, blessings rise,
A holy gift, beneath the skies.

Whispers of Resilience

In silence deep, His whispers come,
A gentle guide, the heartbeats drum.
Through raging storms, the spirit stands,
In faith we rise, with steady hands.

The trials faced, a sacred way,
In pain's embrace, we learn to pray.
Through whispered vows, we find our strength,
With love we journey, through all lengths.

Each setback met, a lesson learned,
In quiet moments, our souls discerned.
To face adversity, with grace we claim,
In whispers soft, we rise the same.

The light within shall not fade out,
Through every shadow, we shall shout.
Resilience born from holy strife,
With every breath, we cherish life.

So let the whispers guide our way,
In faith, we march, to greet the day.
With spirits strong, we shall ascend,
In love and hope, we shall transcend.

Sanctified Through Struggles

In trials faced, our hearts refined,
Through every storm, His love defined.
Beneath the weight, we feel the grace,
In struggles deep, we find our place.

Each challenge met, a sacred trust,
In pain we rise, as purest dust.
With every tear, a blessing sown,
In fractured paths, our strength is grown.

Sanctified by fire and strife,
Through every wound, we uncover life.
With spirits brave and hearts aligned,
In trials faced, true peace we find.

The sacred dance of loss and gain,
In every ache, a love remains.
We walk the path that faith has built,
In every shadow, light is spilt.

Embrace the struggle, hold it dear,
In sacred moments, feel Him near.
For through the trials, we ascend,
Sanctified, our souls shall mend.

In the Shadows of Sacrifice

In shadows cast, the heart must bleed,
For love's pure call, we take the lead.
Each sacrifice, a holy creed,
In darkness found, our spirits freed.

With open hands, we forge the way,
In giving trust, we learn to pray.
Each whispered prayer, a guiding light,
In shadows deep, we find our might.

The burdens bear, we share the pain,
In every loss, our faith remains.
Through sacrifice, the soul takes flight,
In darkest hours, we find the light.

With grateful hearts, we bear the cost,
In love's embrace, we are not lost.
Each choice made, a testament true,
In shadows dwelt, the spirit grew.

So let us walk this sacred line,
In shadows cast, His love we find.
Through sacrifice, we rise anew,
In every heart, a promise due.

Echoes of a Love Worn Thin

In shadows cast by whispers, I walk,
Hearts tattered, yet still we talk.
The echoes linger, a silent plea,
For love once blossomed, now hard to see.

Eclipsed by doubt, our spirits sigh,
Fading warmth beneath the sky.
Yet in the ruins, embers gleam,
A flicker of hope, a fragile dream.

Time steals the joy, but faith remains,
In the solitude of love's refrains.
With heavy hearts, we yearn and strive,
To mend the tapestry of how we thrive.

Through weary steps, we find our grace,
In each other's eyes, a holy space.
In the silence, our souls entwine,
Seeking redemption, a love divine.

Though worn and thin, still we stand,
Each heartbeat echoes, hand in hand.
For in the ashes, we shall find,
Resilience born from love, unconfined.

Baptism by Pain's Grace

In the depths of sorrow, we are washed,
By the tears that forge, the heart once crushed.
Each drop, a lesson, fiercely learned,
In anguish, beauty quietly burned.

Through storms that batter, we emerge anew,
Drenched in compassion, the light breaks through.
With every wound, a story unfolds,
In the tapestry of life, love's truth holds.

Baptized by fire, our spirits gleam,
A journey onward, beyond the dream.
With faith as our anchor, we rise and soar,
Beyond the pain, we are meant for more.

In the embrace of struggle, we find our might,
Each moment a blessing, each shadow a light.
For in the valley of tears, we reclaim,
The strength to redefine our name.

Through trials and trials, our souls expand,
In fragile whispers, we understand.
That pain is a teacher, gentle yet bold,
Revealing the warmth of love untold.

Gathered Fragments of Light

In the twilight's glow, our hearts unite,
Gathered fragments, a dance of light.
From scattered moments, we weave a thread,
Binding the stories of tears we've shed.

Each flicker shines through the veil of night,
Illuminating paths once lost from sight.
In the stillness, wisdom finds its place,
Guiding our spirits with tender grace.

With hands outstretched, we share our dreams,
Mending the seams of love's quiet themes.
In the chorus of hope, our voices blend,
A symphony lifted, where hearts transcend.

Beneath the cosmos, we, too, are one,
Reflecting the journey that's hardly done.
In the hush of grace, we linger near,
Gathered in love, banishing fear.

For every fragment carries a spark,
Illuminating our way from the dark.
In the embrace of the sacred night,
We find our solace in gathered light.

Transcendence in Tear-Streaked Souls

In the still of the night, our sorrow speaks,
Tear-streaked souls, humbled, yet unique.
With every drop, we glimpse the divine,
A path of healing in every line.

Through the valleys low, we long for grace,
Finding strength in our frail embrace.
In the silence, a whisper calls,
Transcending pain, we rise from falls.

Worn by the battles, we carve our fate,
In the hands of love, we resonate.
The scars we bear are marks of flight,
Embracing shadows to seek the light.

In the echoes of anguish, we find our song,
Together we tread, where we belong.
For each tear shed breaks the chains,
Revealing the truth that love remains.

In this sacred journey, we learn to soar,
Transcendence found, forevermore.
With tear-streaked souls, we'll forge ahead,
In the warmth of compassion, we are led.

Legacy of the Resilient

In shadow's grasp, yet we arise,
With faith like mountains, we touch the skies.
Each trial faced, our spirits grow,
Together bound, through fire we glow.

A tapestry woven, strong and bright,
Every thread a story, a guiding light.
Through storms we march, unwavering, bold,
In the heart of struggle, our truth unfolds.

From ashes born, our voices sing,
Embracing hardships, new hope we bring.
In unity fierce, we find our ways,
The legacy built, in love's warm blaze.

With every step, we lift the weak,
In words of kindness, the strong do speak.
A fortress formed from hearts entwined,
The legacy of those who dared to find.

In silent moments, we seek the call,
Listening deeply, we rise and fall.
In the eyes of others, the fire gleams,
Beneath the surface, we share our dreams.

The Divine Craft of Healing

In tender hands, the heart is mended,
With gentle grace, all wounds can end.
Each tear a drop of sacred rain,
In each release, we find our gain.

The broken pieces, like stardust fly,
Transformed by love, we learn to try.
With every touch, the spirit wakes,
In whispered prayers, our solace makes.

A balm for souls is love's embrace,
In unity, we find our place.
Through darkest nights, the light appears,
In shared compassion, we ease our fears.

Miracles unfold in the quiet hum,
With faith ignited, we surely come.
In every heartbeat, the sacred echoes,
The divine craft of healing flows.

From sorrow's depths, we rise anew,
In every moment, the light shines through.
Together we walk, through trials grand,
In the dance of healing, hand in hand.

Murmurs of Redeemed Sorrows

In shadows cast, our sorrows lie,
Yet in their midst, our spirits sigh.
With whispers soft, the heart reveals,
The sacred truth that sorrow heals.

Beneath the weight, hope starts to breathe,
In every struggle, we learn to weave.
The tapestry stitched with tears of grace,
Each thread a story, a holy place.

When darkness lingers, we seek the light,
In every dawn, we find our fight.
Through trials faced, we stand as one,
In redeemed sorrows, our journey's begun.

The echoes of past, a gentle guide,
With every heartbeat, we set aside.
Through pain transformed, our hearts declare,
In murmured prayers, we're always there.

For in our depths, redemption waits,
With each embrace, the soul celebrates.
In every sorrow, a joy concedes,
The murmurs of love, in hope, proceeds.

The Holy Canvas of Experience

On life's vast canvas, colors blend,
With every stroke, new messages send.
Each moment captured, a sacred piece,
In every challenge, we find release.

As seasons change, the palette shifts,
In joy and sorrow, our spirit lifts.
With grace entwined, we paint the skies,
In vibrant hues, the heart complies.

The brush of time, both fierce and kind,
Its whispers guide us, as we unwind.
In strokes of love, our stories bloom,
On this holy canvas, we chase the gloom.

Through laughter shared and lessons learned,
In every heartbeat, a vision burned.
With every fall, we find our rise,
The holy canvas, where wisdom lies.

In unity's dance, our colors twirl,
Together creating a wondrous swirl.
In the embrace of life, we find our thread,
On the holy canvas, our souls are fed.

Praise from the Pain

In shadows deep, where sorrows dwell,
I lift my voice, proclaiming well.
For every wound and heavy chain,
There blooms a grace that frees from pain.

Through trials fierce, my spirit grows,
In faith I stand, despite the throes.
Each tear a testament to light,
From darkness comes a heart so bright.

With weary limbs, I seek the path,
In humble love, I bow to wrath.
Yet in the hurt, I find my song,
A melody where I belong.

From ashes rise, a phoenix true,
In sacred fire, I'll start anew.
With hands uplifted, I shall sing,
My pain transformed, to praise I bring.

The Revelation of Resilience

From brokenness, the spirit plots,
In trials faced, the truth is sought.
With every fall, I learn to stand,
A heart of courage, bold and grand.

When shadows loom and doubts arise,
I seek the light beyond my sighs.
In moments fraught, my soul takes flight,
On wings of faith, I chase the light.

At dawn, the whispers softly call,
Encouragement in each rise and fall.
For in the struggle, I am made,
A warrior's heart, unafraid.

With every breath, I forge my tale,
In storms I stand, my faith prevail.
The strength within, a sacred trust,
In trials faced, my spirit robust.

So let the days unfold their grace,
With resilience, I embrace each place.
A journey marked by hope and love,
Onward I strive, with eyes above.

Celestial Marks of Battle

In heavens bright, the battles rage,
We lift our hearts, our prayers on page.
Each scar a story, brave and true,
Marks of the strife that we walk through.

With shields of faith, we stand as one,
Guardians of light beneath the sun.
In unity, our voices roar,
A sacred chorus, forevermore.

Through tempests fierce, we find our way,
With stars above, each night and day.
For every mark, a lesson learned,
In every fire, our hearts are burned.

With strength bestowed from realms above,
We fight with grace, and lead with love.
In battles won, our spirits soar,
Celestial signs we can't ignore.

Each tear we shed, a gem in hand,
A testament of where we stand.
With every fight, our faith ignites,
Celestial marks, our guiding lights.

Hymns of the Unsheltered

In open skies, the unsheltered roam,
With dreams in hand, they seek a home.
Through woven paths of hope and fear,
Their voices rise, forever clear.

With every step on rugged ground,
Their stories told, in silence found.
From whispers soft, to shouts of praise,
In every heart, a hymn that plays.

United in the quest for peace,
Through trials faced, their strength won't cease.
In bonds of love, they find their way,
With faith as light, they greet the day.

No walls confine, no chains restrain,
In every loss, they rise again.
Each pain endured, a sacred trust,
In unity, their spirits must.

So let the world behold their song,
A symphony of brave and strong.
In hymns of the unsheltered heart,
A testament to love's true art.

Cherished by the Wounds

In the quiet shadows cast by pain,
We find the strength to rise again.
Each scar a story, each ache a song,
In the heart's garden, we learn to belong.

To cherish the wounds is to embrace the light,
In every struggle, we gain insight.
The cracks in our souls let the love flow,
A testament to growth, a seed we sow.

Through trials faced and fears unveiled,
In the path of sorrow, our faith has sailed.
Every tear a blessing, every cry a prayer,
In unity with the wounded, we find our share.

Let mercy drench the soil of despair,
With hope like blossoms, fragrant in the air.
Together, we rise, stronger and wise,
For in the battlefield, true spirit lies.

Embracing our wounds, we turn to grace,
Finding the beauty in every trace.
With hands held high, we journey on,
Cherished by the wounds, we are reborn.

The Alchemy of Adversity

In fire's embrace, our spirits ignite,
Turning sorrow into sacred light.
From ashes we rise, transformed anew,
The gold of our souls shining through.

Trial by trial, we forge our way,
Every tempest a lesson in dismay.
In darkness we learn to seek the flame,
The alchemy of life, forging our name.

Mountains may tremble, and storms may roar,
Yet in these battles, we find the door.
To wisdom and strength, embracing the storm,
In the heart of adversity, we find our form.

Hope is the thread that weaves through despair,
A tapestry of trials, woven with care.
In each broken piece, a story sings,
The alchemy of life, as suffering brings.

With faith as our compass, we journey on,
From the depths of darkness, a new dawn drawn.
Each challenge faced, a step toward grace,
In the dance of adversity, we find our place.

Emblems of the Enduring Spirit

In the whispers of the ancient trees,
Lie the tales of brave hearts and knees.
Emblems of spirit, resilient and true,
In each life's journey, a miracle renews.

Through storms endured and trials faced,
We gather our courage; it cannot be replaced.
With each heartbeat echoing grace,
We rise like phoenixes, finding our place.

Each scar a medal, each tear a testament,
In the tapestry of life, we find contentment.
Emblems of hope shimmer in the night,
Guiding our spirits to soar and take flight.

The strength of the soul is a weapon fine,
With love as our shield, we forever shine.
In unity, we rise, together we stand,
Emblems of the enduring spirit, hand in hand.

Through shadows we wander, together we leap,
In joy and in sorrow, our promises keep.
With hearts intertwined, our paths we share,
Emblems of faith, forever laid bare.

Sacred Layers of Experience

In each layer of life, a lesson unfolds,
Whispers of wisdom in stories untold.
The tapestry woven, rich and profound,
Sacred experiences in silence resound.

From laughter and tears, we gather our grace,
The seasons of life, a divine embrace.
In the stillness of nights, reflections ignite,
Each moment a treasure, each memory bright.

Through trials and triumphs, in joy, we sway,
The sacred layers guide us on our way.
With patience and love, we peel back the skin,
To reveal our true selves, the light within.

In the caress of wind and the song of the sea,
We find our belonging, at last, we are free.
Every scar and mark tells a story of worth,
Sacred layers of experience, a dance of rebirth.

With humility's heart, we embrace the unknown,
In the journey of life, together, we've grown.
Each layer a promise, a jewel, a prayer,
Sacred experiences forever we share.

Lessons from the Divine Forge

In the heart of fire, souls are formed,
By hands unseen, we are transformed.
Each trial burns, each lesson learned,
In sacred embers, our spirits yearned.

Tempered in faith, like steel we rise,
Through shadows cast, we seek the skies.
With every strike, our purpose clear,
The Divine whispers, "Do not fear."

Each scar a mark, each wound a grace,
In suffering's depths, we find our place.
Forged in love, as one we stand,
Guided by light, led by His hand.

The anvil of life, it shapes our fate,
With patience bestowed, we learn to wait.
From molten dreams, we craft our way,
Embracing the dawn of a brand new day.

In unity of spirit, we find our song,
Through trials faced, we grow strong.
Blessed by the forge, we shine anew,
In divine lessons, we are renewed.

The Covenant of Enduring Faith

A promise whispered, a bond so rare,
Through trials and storms, we lay it bare.
In hearts united, we find our peace,
In faith that flourishes, our doubts cease.

With every heartbeat, His love persists,
A guiding light through life's dark twists.
In joy and sorrow, we lift our voice,
In gratitude's song, we make our choice.

Hands clasped together, a sacred trust,
In bonds unbroken, we rise from dust.
Through seasons shifting, our spirits soar,
The covenant made shall last evermore.

In moments fleeting, His grace bestowed,
Through paths uncertain, our faiths exploded.
With courage summoned, we walk the line,
In the heart of love, our souls intertwine.

As dawn breaks over the endless night,
We stand together, hearts burning bright.
In the flame of hope, we shall endure,
For in His promise, we are secure.

Strength in Shattered Form

In fragments broken, beauty lies,
Through shattered dreams, our spirit flies.
Each piece a story, each scar a song,
In the light of grace, we find where we belong.

With every tear, a lesson learned,
In depths of darkness, our hearts discerned.
The strength we gather from pain and loss,
In every shadow, we bear our cross.

Through the cracks of life, the light pours through,
A testament to all we've made it through.
In unity of sorrow, we grow anew,
And from the ashes, we rise like dew.

In every fracture, a chance to heal,
The gift of faith—a binding seal.
With courage blossoming in stormy days,
We find our purpose, in countless ways.

In shattered form, our hearts stay strong,
Through trials faced, we sing our song.
For in the pieces, there's beauty found,
In strength united, we stand our ground.

Angelic Imprints on the Heart

In the gentle stillness, a whisper calls,
Angelic presence where love enthralls.
Their wings like shadows, wrap us tight,
Guarding our paths, guiding our light.

With every heartbeat, their grace instills,
A sacred knowing that time fulfills.
Through trials faced, they hold us near,
In moments of doubt, they quell our fear.

In softest gestures, their love can sway,
In kindness shown, they light the way.
Each interaction, a heavenly plan,
Imprints of angels, the heart understands.

In laughter shared, in tears we weep,
Their presence lingers, soul-deep.
In every touch, their story spins,
A tapestry woven of where love begins.

So listen closely, to the heart's refrain,
For angelic imprints shall never wane.
In the fabric of life, they gently weave,
A testament of love that we believe.

Chiseled by Divinity's Hand

In the clay of our being, we are shaped,
By whispers of glory, unbreakably draped.
Each mark that we bear tells a tale of grace,
Crafted in love, in this sacred space.

Every struggle endured, a notch on our soul,
Sculpted by fires, to make us whole.
The chisel of time, though it may seem stern,
For beauty emerges in each twist and turn.

With patience divine, our essence is refined,
In the heart of the storm, a purpose aligned.
Each flaw that we see becomes part of the plan,
For we are all touched by the hand of the man.

Through shadows and light, we dance in the pain,
Awakening strength like drops of the rain.
Transformed in the forge, where struggle is fate,
We rise from the ashes, our spirit sedate.

In moments of doubt, let faith take its stand,
For there is a reason we're chiseled by hand.
Embrace every curve, every jagged edge,
For in our imperfections, we honor the pledge.

Grace in the Cracks of Skin

In the valleys of sorrow where shadows reside,
Emerges a beauty that cannot hide.
Through scars and through wounds, grace finds its way,
In cracks of our skin, it dances to stay.

Each whisper of pain, a story unfolds,
Of redemption and hope, like the sun's golden folds.
For the heart that has broken can feel more than most,
In the depths of despair, we find what we boast.

Grace flows like rivers through roughened terrain,
Awakening spirits from slumber and pain.
With each tear that falls, a blessing takes flight,
Illuminated softly by the promise of light.

In shadows of doubt, love reaches its hand,
Through life's jagged edges, we bravely will stand.
For every imperfection, a canvas divine,
In the cracks of our skin, pure grace shall align.

So let us embrace all the trials we face,
For beauty and grace are one with our pace.
In the tapestry woven, our lives intertwine,
Each thread is a testament, sacred and fine.

The Silent Testament of Trials

In silence we journey, through valleys of doubt,
Each step a testament, each whisper a shout.
For trials that bind us are paths to our heart,
In the quiet of struggle, we learn who we are.

The weight of the world collapses our pride,
Yet in every burden, strength must abide.
Through tears that we shed, wisdom takes flight,
A beacon of hope in the darkest of night.

And though we may falter, we rise with the dawn,
In the arms of our faith, we carry on.
For every storm weathered, each wound that we bear,
Is a silent testament that whispers in prayer.

With humility graced, we walk ancient roads,
Collecting our stories like luminous loads.
In the tapestry woven with threads of our fears,
Lives the silent testament of our silent years.

Each trial a teacher, each scar a wise friend,
Reminding our spirits that we shall transcend.
In the sacred embrace of our struggles, we find,
The solace of truth in the depths of the mind.

Crowned with Imperfections

Upon our heads rest crowns made of flaws,
Each jagged edge draws us closer to pause.
For in our imperfections, we find our worth,
A holy reflection of our place on Earth.

With every mistake, a lesson we gain,
Each stumble and fall, a chance to sustain.
For grace walks beside us in laughter and tears,
Crowning our efforts, dispelling our fears.

In the mirror of life, we see not defeat,
But beauty unfiltered, our journey complete.
For flawed could be perfect, as hearts learn to sing,
In echoes of love, the joy that we bring.

So, wear that crown brightly, let others behold,
The strength that is woven in stories retold.
For we are the tapestry, rich and alive,
Crowned with imperfections, beautifully thrive.

In humble acceptance, our spirits shall soar,
Finding grace in the cracks, and love evermore.
So lift up your head and rejoice in this plan,
For crowned we walk forward, hand in hand.

Sacred Resilience

In shadows deep, the faithful stand,
Hearts held high, in God's strong hand.
Through trials fierce, our spirits soar,
With every struggle, we rise once more.

Faith a beacon, shining bright,
Guiding souls through darkest night.
In whispers soft, we hear His call,
A sacred promise, never to fall.

In unity, we find our grace,
Together we run this holy race.
With every step, our purpose clear,
Sacred resilience conquers fear.

When storms arise, and doubts abound,
In prayerful hearts, strength is found.
For in His love, we are awakened,
Boundless hope, eternally unshaken.

Each breath a hymn, each heartbeat prayer,
In divine presence, we forever stare.
With faith as armor, we face the strife,
In sacred resilience, we embrace life.

Whispers of Endurance

In silent prayer, we find our way,
Through trials fierce, and shadows gray.
With steadfast hearts, we walk the line,
Embracing strength, a gift divine.

Through every trial, we stand tall,
In whispers soft, we heed His call.
With courage clothed in faith's embrace,
Endurance leads us to His grace.

The journey long, but spirits bright,
With loving guides, we find the light.
In every tear, a lesson learned,
In every flame, our souls discerned.

Like flickering stars in the vast night,
We shine with hope, a radiant sight.
For in each struggle, a testament true,
Whispers of endurance lead us through.

The strength of heart, the hope we share,
In divine truth, beyond compare.
Together we rise, in faith's embrace,
With whispers of endurance, we find our place.

Transcendence in Tribulation

In shadows deep, our spirits soar,
Through troubled waters, we seek more.
In every trial, a truth unfolds,
Transcendence found, in hearts so bold.

Through pain and sorrow, grace abides,
In the divine, our hope resides.
With every tear, a seed of light,
Transcendence blooms, dispelling night.

In unity, our voices blend,
A symphony where sorrows mend.
For in our hearts, the Savior's song,
Transcendence rises, oh, so strong.

With faith unyielding, we embrace the fight,
In tribulation, we find our sight.
Bound by love, we journey far,
Transcendence shines, our guiding star.

Each challenge faced, a step of grace,
Through struggles hard, we find our place.
In faith eternal, we stand renewed,
Transcendence blooms, our spirits imbued.

The Divine Forge

In the heart of trials, the furnace glows,
In each challenge faced, our spirit grows.
Through heat and pressure, we are refined,
The divine forge shapes heart and mind.

With every strike, our purpose clear,
In faith's embrace, we conquer fear.
Forged in love, we rise anew,
The divine forge, a path for you.

Each moment tested, a sacred grace,
Through fires of life, we find our place.
In every struggle, strength shall bloom,
The divine forge dispels all gloom.

With iron will, and hearts that soar,
We walk in light, forevermore.
Embracing change, we learn, we grow,
In the divine forge, our spirits glow.

Through darkest nights, we'll see the dawn,
In every trial, a rebirth drawn.
For in the flames, true beauty lies,
The divine forge, where hope never dies.

The Pilgrim's Trail of Hardships

In shadows deep, the path we tread,
With faith our guide, through tears we bled.
Each stone and thorn, a test divine,
Yet closer to the light we shine.

The winds may howl, the nights may chill,
But in our hearts, we find the will.
With every step, our spirits soar,
In search of grace, forevermore.

Though trials come like stormy seas,
We raise our hands with earnest pleas.
For on this trail, we seek the truth,
As sages speak, we find our youth.

The mountains high, the valleys low,
In faith we rise, in love we grow.
Each struggle made, a prayer in time,
Our souls uplifted, hearts in rhyme.

So let us walk, with courage bold,
The sacred journey, ours to hold.
Through every grief, through every trial,
We stride in hope, and grace we smile.

Embers of the Soul's Reverence

From ashes rise the dreams of old,
In quiet night, their stories told.
A flicker bright, amidst the gloom,
Embers dance, dispelling doom.

In sacred space, where silence dwells,
The whispers rise, the spirit swells.
With every breath, a hymn of grace,
We seek the light in this holy place.

The heart ignites with passion's flame,
In each struggle, we find our name.
Through trials faced, our souls refined,
In every scar, our truth enshrined.

Oh, let the embers softly glow,
In reverence, our spirits grow.
For in this light, we learn to see,
The sacred ties that set us free.

With love as guide, we journey on,
Through every dusk, into the dawn.
With every flame, a prayer shall soar,
Embers of soul, forevermore.

Healing in Holy Ruins

In ruins old, where whispers stay,
The echoes of the past will sway.
With broken walls, our hearts repair,
In healing grace, we find our prayer.

The stones may sigh of battles lost,
Yet hope emerges, no matter the cost.
Through cracks and crevices, light will flow,
In holy ruins, new life will grow.

With every wound, a story shared,
In community, we're all ensnared.
Together we rise, hand in hand,
In sacred moments, we understand.

The tempest shook, but faith remains,
In shattered dreams, our love sustains.
From brokenness, a tapestry spun,
In holy ruins, we are one.

So let us gather, hearts aligned,
In healing fields, our souls entwined.
For in the rubble, there's beauty found,
In holy ruins, hope resounds.

The Blessing of Battle Scars

In every mark, a story told,
Of battles fought, of courage bold.
Each scar a sign of trials faced,
In every wound, a heart embraced.

The struggle shapes the soul's design,
In every bruise, a strength divine.
Through tempests fierce, we learned to rise,
With battle scars, we touch the skies.

Each scratch, each line, a map of grace,
In every trial, we find our place.
For in the pain, the wisdom grows,
The blessing of scars, a gift that glows.

So lift your eyes, embrace the fight,
For in the dark, we seek the light.
With every battle, a sacred art,
The blessing of scars, our life's sweet heart.

And when we falter, when we break,
Our scars remind us, the path we make.
In unity, we find our way,
With battle scars, we rise and stay.

Reclaiming the Remnants

In the shadows of despair, light breaks through,
Calling forth the lost, the weary, the true.
Gathering the fragments, He makes us whole,
In shattered places, He ignites the soul.

Whispers of grace in the silence surround,
Binding the wounds that time had unbound.
From ashes to beauty, a journey we tread,
In reclaiming the remnants, hope's thread is spread.

With hands lifted high, we surrender the past,
Embracing new life, the die has been cast.
Each tear that we shed, a pearl of the night,
In reclaiming our spirits, we soar to the light.

Through valleys of shadows, His promise resounds,
In faith we find strength, where love abounds.
The remnants of sorrow, transformed into song,
In the heart of the faithful, we each belong.

Reclaiming the remnants, our destinies blend,
In communion with grace, our hearts we extend.
Together we rise, united as one,
In the dance of redemption, we shine like the sun.

The Parable of the Broken Road

Upon the broken road, weary feet tread,
Walking through shadows, where angels fear to spread.
Every stone tells a tale, every crack holds a truth,
In the journey of life, we reclaim our youth.

Lessons in struggle, the soul's gentle guide,
Faith lights the way, through the storms we bide.
In every detour, a grace to behold,
The parable whispers of treasures untold.

With each passing moment, the heart learns to see,
That the broken road leads to eternity.
In the tapestry woven of trials and strife,
We find the rich fabric of our sacred life.

Every stumble and fall, a step towards the light,
In the depths of our sorrow, we find our respite.
The road may be rugged, but He walks beside,
In the parable's lesson, we shall abide.

So let us embrace the path that we roam,
For even in brokenness, we are never alone.
Each mark in the dust tells the story we've told,
In the parable of life, our spirits unfold.

Sacred Marks of Endurance

With sacred marks, our journeys align,
Carved deep in the heart, their stories divine.
Every trial endured, a testament strong,
In the depths of our being, we each belong.

These sacred markings, like stars in the night,
Guide weary souls with their luminous light.
They tell of the battles, the struggles we've faced,
In the tapestry of life, each thread interlaced.

In moments of silence, their whispers resound,
In the echoes of grace, true strength can be found.
For every scar treasured, a lesson bestowed,
In the sacred marks of endurance, we've grown.

Together we gather, with open hearts wide,
Embracing the journey, with love as our guide.
Hand in hand we walk, through valleys and peaks,
In the sacred marks of endurance, our spirit speaks.

Through storm and through calm, we shall always rise,
In the face of our fears, we find the skies.
With sacred marks upon us, forever we stand,
In the legacy of love, united, we band.

Chapters Inked in Heart's Ink

In pages unturned, our stories begin,
With chapters inked boldly, where faith draws us in.
Each line a reflection of lessons we've learned,
In the heart's sacred ink, our spirits have burned.

From whispers of hope to cries of despair,
In the ink of our hearts, the truth we lay bare.
With each joyful triumph and sorrowful night,
Our stories unfold in the warmth of His light.

Ink flows like rivers, in shadows and sun,
With every new chapter, the journey's begun.
Each moment a canvas, painted with grace,
In the heart's vibrant ink, we find our true place.

Together we gather, in stories we weave,
In the chapters of life, we learn to believe.
With love as our compass, and faith as our sail,
In the heart's inked chapters, we shall never fail.

So let us embrace every twist and each turn,
For in the heart's ink, our spirits will burn.
With chapters that echo the songs of the divine,
In the tale of our lives, His light will shine.

Milton Keynes UK
Ingram Content Group UK Ltd.
UKHW031320271124
451618UK00007B/187